TABLE OF CONTENTS

	PAGE
INTRODUCTION	1
ACCOUNTING OVERVIEW	1
LEGAL CONSIDERATIONS AND ACCESS TO RECORDS	11
CONDUCTING FINANCIAL INTERVIEWS	17
DIRECT METHODS OF TRACING FINANCIAL TRANSACTIONS	28
INDIRECT METHODS OF TRACING FINANCIAL TRANSACTIONS	43
STATISTICAL SAMPLING	54

FINANCIAL INVESTIGATIONS
and the
TRACING of FUNDS

FC 19-149

PALADIN PRESS
BOULDER, COLORADO

Financial Investigations and the Tracing of Funds
Copyright © 1990 by Paladin Press

ISBN 0-87364-549-9
Printed in the United States of America

Published by Paladin Press, a division of
Paladin Enterprises, Inc., P.O. Box 1307,
Boulder, Colorado 80306, USA.
(303) 443-7250

Direct inquiries and/or orders to the above address.

All rights reserved. Except for use in a review, no
portion of this book may be reproduced in any form
without the express written permission of the publisher.

Neither the author nor the publisher assumes
any responsibility for the use or misuse of
information contained in this book.

INTRODUCTION

The Army's continuing war on drugs, the ever-present problem of loss of government property, and the growing emphasis on eliminating fraud, waste, and abuse in the military sector, ensure that crimes for profit will constitute a significant part of the investigator's workload. You should not consider the investigation or preparation of these cases complete until the techniques described in this field circular have been considered and appropriately utilized. By following the steps for tracing funds, conducting financial interviews, and using legal weapons at your disposal, you increase the likelihood of a successful investigation.

This field circular may be used in conjunction with FC 19-146 (Computer-Related Crime) if an automated system is used for the purpose of financial accountability.

ACCOUNTING OVERVIEW

Accounting is more than three thousand years old. Stone and clay tablets containing financial records have been discovered by archeologists in several locations throughout the world. The Roman Empire developed methods of recording and summarizing numerical information. The Romans maintained elaborate records for such purposes as keeping track of their military personnel and their military payroll. The American Indian used notches on sticks and strings of beads to denote the accumulation of data.

The art of accounting evolved slowly over thousands of years until trade and business reached a complexity which required something more sophisticated. During the Industrial Revolution in Europe, large pools of capital were needed to finance the purchase of machinery and equipment. Partnerships, joint-stock companies, and corporations evolved to meet this need. New accounting procedures had to be developed for these new business organizations.

While the art of accounting is very old, the profession of accounting, in comparison to other professions, is extremely young.

ACCOUNTING PERSONNEL

As accounting became more sophisticated, so did the people who used it. Thus it becomes important to the investigator that he or she have some understanding of the duties and functions of the accounting personnel who may be encountered during an investigation. This will assist you, as an investigator, in knowing who to ask what questions.

The internal accounting staff can be viewed as a three-tiered hierarchy. At the top is the principal responsible financial officer. This person may have the title of President, Vice President, Treasurer or Comptroller. At any rate, when making initial contact, it is a good policy to seek out the principal financial officer to obtain approval and cooperation. An initial approach at any other level will probably elicit the response "Sorry, we don't give out that information."

The principal financial officer generally will pass you along to the second level, the chief accountant who heads the accounting staff. From this person you can obtain general information about the accounting system, where the records are located, and who is most familiar with them. In the event you are running down some particular item or type of account, the chief accountant will turn you over to the next level, the accounting or posting clerks. These employees are most familiar with the day-to-day entries to the books of account. They can be a big help in tracing items in the books.

Many businesses employ outside accountants whose responsibility is to audit the books and verify the accuracy of a company's financial statements. These outside accountants are generally certified public accountants (CPAs) who are licensed and regulated by each state. If for some reason the records of a company are out of reach, it may be possible to get the information sought from interviewing the CPA and examining his or her workpapers.

During the course of an independent audit, the CPA sends letters to customers, creditors, and lending institutions to verify sales, receipts, outstanding balances and cash transactions of the company. These documents are only a part of the CPA's workpapers. They also contain analyses of the company's individual ledger accounts, comments on internal control, and various computations that become a permanent part of the CPA's workpapers. Your review of all of these workpapers could provide valuable leads as well as documentary evidence.

DEFINITION OF ACCOUNTING

A professional accounting association has defined accounting as the act of recording, classifying, and summarizing money transactions and events of a financial nature, and interpreting the results thereof.

FORMS OF BUSINESS ORGANIZATION

The proprietorship, also called sole proprietorship, is the simplest to set up and is the most common business form. Usually no legal red tape is involved--proprietor just commences business. BUT, a license may be required to engage in a particular activity (regardless of whether it is done by proprietorship, partnership, or corporation), such as funeral home, liquor store, or restaurant.

A partnership is created when two or more persons agree to do business together. In a general partnership each partner has authority to participate in the management of the business, although the partnership agreement may divide the management in specific ways (one person handling sales, another bookkeeping). Profits and losses are usually divided equally, although the agreement may specify another division of profits or losses.

A corporation is an entity legally separate from the persons owning it. Corporations are created by state governments (in a few cases, also by the federal government). Actions taken by a corporation are restricted to what is permitted by state corporate law and what is authorized by the charter of the corporation. A corporation is owned by its stockholders (also called shareholders), who hold stock (also called shares) in the corporation. A corporation can own property, buy, sell, enter into contracts, borrow money or take any other business action an individual can take, subject always to the limitations imposed by law and by the corporation's charter.

A limited partnership permits partners to limit their risk to the amount of their investment. Their risk is similar to the limited liability of a stockholder of a corporation. A limited partnership agreement must be in writing (usually a copy of the agreement is filed in the county courthouse, as required by most State laws). There must be at least one general partner, who has unlimited liability. Limited partners may not participate in the management of the firm, although they may meet from time to time to vote on general policies of operation. This form has recently been popular in oil drilling, cattle feeding, and real estate ventures.

A cooperative is a corporation in which profits are distributed to shareholders not in proportion to the number of shares each owns, but in proportion to the amount of business each shareholder (also called member) does with the cooperative. Unlike a business corporation, which generally allows one vote per share, a cooperative allows one vote per member.

A mutual company is a type of corporation that has no stockholders. It is common in the fields of life insurance and savings. It is owned by its customers (policyholders of depositors), who may or may not have the right to vote for the directors, depending on the provisions of the charter. If any profits are distributed, they are paid out according to the size of the policy or the size of the deposit.

COMPARISON OF FORMS OF BUSINESS ORGANIZATION

SOLE PROPRIETORSHIP	GENERAL PARTNERSHIP	CORPORATION
Advantages	*Advantages*	*Advantages*
Ownership of all profits	Larger capital resources than sole proprietorship	Limited liability of stockholders
Ease of organization	Better credit standing than single individual	Very large capital resources possible
Freedom of action	More managerial talent than single individual	Ease of transfer of ownership
Minimum of legal restrictions	Few legal restrictions	Long or perpetual life
Maximum personal incentive	High degree of personal incentive	Ease of expansion
Freedom from tax on business income	Freedom from tax on business income	Legal entity distinct from owners
Ease of dissolution	Ease of dissolution	
Disadvantages	*Disadvantages*	*Disadvantages*
Unlimited liability for business debts	Unlimited liability for business debts	Tax on business income
Limited capital resources	Existence ends with death or withdrawal of any partner	Extensive legal restrictions and regulations
Life of business ends with death of proprietor	Restricted transfer of ownership	Expenses of organization
		Possibly limited personal incentive

If Company A holds enough voting stock in Company B to control Company B, Company A is called a holding company (also called the parent company) and Company B is called a subsidiary of Company A. By controlling Company B, Company A can borrow money from Company B at attractive terms (such loans are called upstream loans), sell to Company B at attractive prices or buy at low prices, and enjoy various other benefits. If Company B becomes bankrupt, Company A loses only its investment in stock in Company B, as do other stockholders, if any, holding Company B stock.

A shell corporation is one that has no assets or liabilities. It simply has a charter to do business. Attractions of shell corporations are speed and confidentiality. Original application may take weeks to approve. Names of persons on the original application for charter to the state government are on record with the secretary of state and may be investigated before a charter is issued. Names of subsequent stockholders and directors are not on record with the secretary of state.

SYSTEMS

The ultimate object of any accounting system is to show, in summary form, the results of transactions. This can be done in many ways. We will discuss the two systems most commonly used: single-entry bookkeeping and double-entry bookkeeping.

Single-Entry Bookkeeping

This is the system that has been used for most of the three thousand years of accounting. It is the simplest form of noting a financial transaction. With the advent of more complex financial organizations, it has declined in use. However, it is still in use by some small businesses. In its most sophisticated form, it is merely the entering of information from all sources in one place--usually in columnar form. In other words, it is a system of accounting for financial transactions without making an effort to balance the records.

Double-Entry Bookkeeping

This concept in accounting is that every transaction affects two or more accounts with equal debits and credits and is recorded in them. Thus two or more adjustments must be made, never just one. The name "double entry" is derived from this fact.

The object of the double entry system is to show, in summary form, the results of the many transactions and forces affecting a business. To do this requires an organized and convenient system for classifying all business transactions.

THE FUNDAMENTAL EQUATION

The basic concept of the double-entry system is that every item of value of whatever kind is owned or claimed by someone. This may be expressed in the form of an equation.

Items of Value = Claims

Items of Value

The various things owned by a company are called assets. They include cash, supplies, machinery, furniture, fixtures, land, and other tangible things too numerous to mention. There are other assets which are not physical things, such as the right to collect money from others, patents, investments, goodwill, and the like. To be treated as an asset, the item should be of value to the owner; if it has no value to the owner, it is not the concern of the accounting system.

Claims

There are two kinds of claims against the assets. The first is the claim of the owners for the total value invested. This is called equity, capital, or net worth. This represents the original investment of the owners of a business minus any losses sustained plus any profits retained in the business. In a proprietorship all of the net worth belongs to the proprietor. In a partnership the share of the net worth belonging to each partner is designated. In a corporation the net worth is divided into at least two accounts—capital stock and surplus (or retained earnings). The capital stock account may be divided into preferred stock and common stock.

The second kind of claim arises from those who extended credit to the business. Such claims may be from suppliers, banks, investors, mortgages, and the like. The claims of these creditors are known as liabilities.

The previous equation can now be converted to the fundamental accounting equation.

Assets = Liabilities + Capital

A = L + C

Although business transactions affect the composition of one or more of the items in the equation, the total of assets must always equal the total of claims. If the equation is to be maintained, it is impossible to change a single item alone without destroying it. For instance, when an asset is increased, a corresponding adjustment must be made in the equation or it will not balance; either another asset must be decreased, or a liability or net worth increased.

The following table classifies the effects of any business transaction under double-entry bookkeeping:

THE CHANGE	THE RESULT
Increase in an asset	Decrease in another asset, or Increase in a liability, or Increase in an item of net worth.
Decrease in an asset	Increase in another asset, or Decrease in a liability, or Decrease in an item of net worth.
Increase in a liability	Decrease in another liability, or Increase in an asset, or Decrease in an item of net worth.
Decrease in a liability	Increase in another liability, or Decrease in an asset, or Increase in an item of net worth.
Increase in an item of net worth	Increase in an asset, or Decrease in a liability, or Decrease in another item of net worth.
Decrease in an item of net worth	Decrease in an asset, or Increase in a liability, or Increase in another item of net worth.

All of these transactions are classified into various types of accounts. An account is a heading, or title, pertaining to the various assets, the various liabilities, or factors which affect net worth. The increases and decreases resulting from business transactions expressed in terms of money are recorded in two columns under each of these account headings. The column on the left is called the debit column and the column on the right is called the credit column. "Debit" refers only to the left column of an account; "credit" to the right column. The rules for recording the increases and decreases resulting from the transactions are as follows:

Assets

Increases on the left   Decreases on the right
    (debit)   (credit)
Normal balance

Liabilities and Net Worth (Capital)

Decreases on the left   Increases on the right
    (debit)   (credit)
                                       Normal balance

Income

Decreases on the left   Increases on the right
    (debit)   (credit)
                                       Normal balance

Expenses

Increases on the left   Decreases on the right
    (debit)   (credit)
Normal balance

In analyzing transactions, the following steps should be taken in conformity with the above rule:

° Determine the accounts affected by the transaction.

° Determine the effect on each account; that is, increase or decrease.

° Apply the appropriate designation in the account; that is, debit or credit.

EXAMPLES OF DEBIT OR CREDIT BOOK ENTRIES

Example 1

Company Y buys a desk for $200, paying cash.

ENTRY:

CASH				
	PR	DR	CR	BAL
				$ 500
		$200		300

FURNITURE				
	PR	DR	CR	BAL
				$6000
		$ 200		6200

Example 2

Company Y buys a desk for $200, paying $50 cash and $150 on account.

ENTRY:

FURNITURE				
	PR	DR	CR	BAL
				$6000
		$200		6200

CASH				
	PR	DR	CR	BAL
				$ 500
			$ 50	450

ACCT'S PAYABLE				
	PR	DR	CR	BAL
				$ 400
			$150	550

Example 3

Company Y sells $2,000 in merchandise; $500 in cash is paid by the customer C.O.D. and balance is to be paid on account.

ENTRY:

CASH				
	PR	DR	CR	BAL
				$ 600
		$ 500		1,100

ACCT'S RECEIVABLE				
	PR	DR	CR	BAL
				$ 950
		$1,500		2,450

SALES				
	PR	DR	CR	BAL
				$17,000
			$2,000	19,000

A _final note_ - "Anything that is recorded as a debit (credit) in one set of books _is recorded_ as a credit (debit) in somebody else's books."

METHODS

There are two methods of accounting: cash basis and accrual basis. However, there are three ways that these methods can be used:

° Cash basis only.

° Accrual basis only.

° A combination of these methods, called the hybrid method.

Cash basis means that revenues are recorded in the period when the cash collections are received and that the expenses are recorded in the period when the cash is paid out. NOTE: The "pivotal" words are "received" and "paid." In other words, only when you physically have received the collection--not the promise to pay--or have paid the expense do you have the basis for making an entry in the books.)

Accrual basis means that revenues are recorded in the period earned (regardless of when collected) and expenses are recorded in the period incurred (regardless of when cash was disbursed).

The fundamental difference between the cash and accrual basis is in the matter of "timing." Acountants often describe the process of determining periodical net income as a proper "matching" of revenues and expenses by periods. This is achieved by the accrual basis of accounting. It is not achieved by the cash basis of accounting except for those transactions that normally are completed within the given period.

Example 4

You order $500 worth of widgets to use for heating in December for delivery in December. However, you do not pay for the widgets until January.

Cash basis method: You would record the $500 as an expense when paid in January.

Accrual basis method: You would record the $500 as an expense when incurred (or committed for) in December.

Example 5

You are in the business of tree removal. You receive an order in April to remove a tree. You remove the tree for $190 in April, but the customer does not pay you until June.

Cash basis method: You would record the receipt of the the $190 as income in your books in June when you received the payment.

Accrual basis method: You would record the $190 as income in April when it was earned.

The hybrid method of accounting is a combination of the cash-basis and accrual-basis methods. It can be used if it is consistently applied and clearly reflects income. It is most commonly used when inventories (items held for resale) are involved. In a small business, it simplifies the recordkeeping because, in determining net income, only sales and cost of sales accounts are recorded on the accrual basis, while all other accounts are kept on the cash basis. In a small business, the "timing" of incurring expenses and paying them is usually of short duration. There is little distortion of net income; thus, in these circumstances it is an acceptable method. However, it is not acceptable to use the cash basis for recording income, and accural basis for recording expenses because the distortion could be material.

When investigating a small business, you may find it uses the hybrid method for recording transactions. Larger businesses, as a rule, will use the accrual basis method because of the volume and complexity of recording the transactions, and because of such management practices as making future business projections, analyzing cash flow through the business, and realistically costing their product or service.

THE BALANCE SHEET

To understand the complete accounting cycle, you would begin by studying the balance sheet. The balance sheet is a financial statement depicting at a specific time and in a systematic manner the assets (A), liabilities (L), and capital (C) of a business organization. The fundamental equation A = L + C can also be stated A - L = C.

10

LEGAL CONSIDERATIONS AND ACCESS TO RECORDS

An extremely valuable line of investigation frequently overlooked by trial counsel and military investigators is an analysis of the finances of a suspect or suspect group. There are a variety of investigative tools available that will allow the government to review a person's current and past financial transactions, so as to detect possible illegal income. Such review can be particularly useful in investigating any crime involving an economic motive. For example, large unexplainable cash deposits can help to distinguish drug dealers from drug users and to identify persons involved in the large scale, systematic theft of government property. Trial counsel should have at least a general familiarity with the techniques for obtaining bank records, tax returns, and corporate books so as to enable them to follow the money obtained from illegal activity.

Access to personal financial records can be obtained through the following techniques:

° Formal request to the suspect.

° Military or federal search warrant.

° Administrative subpoena.

° Court ordered access (applicable to tax records, credit reports, and grand jury materials).

FORMAL REQUEST TO THE SUSPECT

The functional equivalent of a consent search, this is the simplest and easiest method of access to financial records. This method is frequently overlooked because of the logical, but often false assumption, that suspects would never give their consent. Quite the contrary, many suspects will quickly grant the government access to their financial records. There are a variety of reasons for this. The most obvious is that those suspects who are innocent have nothing to hide and have a vested interest in having the focus of the investigation shifted away from them. Even those suspects who have actually committed an offense will frequently grant access out of arrogance or general lack of mental acumen. This technique can be particularly advantageous when you are trying to narrow the range of suspects from a relatively large group such as a company or platoon. Merely knowing which unit members choose not to give consent may in itself be of significant investigative value. Another significant advantage of this technique is that the government does not need a prerequisite quantum of proof concerning the commission of a crime prior to its use.

JUDICIAL SEARCH WARRANT

Like any other piece of evidence, financial records can be obtained through the use of a judicial search warrant. These warrants can be served on either the suspect or on any third party, such as a financial institution, accountant, or tax preparer, who might have copies of the records sought. As a general rule, search warrants from a military judge or magistrate can be used to obtain financial records from any office or institution located on a military installation. Records maintained off-post may be obtained through the use of a federal search warrant. Access to these warrants was facilitated by a revision to the regulations interpreting Rule 41, Search Warrant, of the Federal Rules of Criminal Procedure. Army CID agents are now considered federal law enforcement officers for the purposes of requesting search warrants. While prior coordination with an assistant US attorney is required, Army CID agents are now authorized to directly request the issuance of search warrants from federal district court judges. CID agents are authorized to execute these warrants in furtherance of investigations within their jurisdiction.

The obvious limiting factor to the use of a judicial warrant is the probable cause requirement.

ADMINISTRATIVE SUBPOENA

Army CID personnel are authorized to request the use of the Department of Defense Inspector General (DODIG) subpoena. This administrative subpoena authority was established by Section 6(a)(4) of the Inspector General Act of 1978, and Title 5, US Code, App. III, Sec. 1-12 (1982), and became available to DOD investigators with the creation of the DODIG in 1982. This subpoena can be used to obtain records and documents relevant to military investigators from businesses, financial institutions, individuals, and state and local governmental agencies. This subpoena cannot be used to obtain records from federal agencies. An interesting use of this subpoena is to force the production of a suspect's tax records from the suspect himself. This is an alternate method of obtaining tax records and is faster than the court-ordered procedure described later in this FC.

Trial counsel who wish to use this subpoena should forward their requests through their local CID offices to HQ, USACIDC, ATTN: Operations Directorate, Economic Crime Division.

The key advantage to the use of the DODIG subpoena is its extremely broad scope. It can be used to compel the production of nonprivileged documentary evidence from any source other than a federal agency. Its investigatory power is not limited to military installations. There is no prerequisite quantum of proof as to the commission of a crime by a particular person. The only essential requirement for the use of this administrative subpoena is that the information sought be relevant to the legitimate operational concerns of the Defense Department.

Requests for access to the administrative subpoena are granted at the discretion of the DODIG. As a practical matter, this subpoena has been most often used in cases involving some type of fraud. There have been exceptions, however. For example, recently the DODIG subpoena was used to further a homicide investigation. It is important to note that investigations utilizing the DODIG subpoena are technically assumed under the operational control of the DODIG.

ACCESS TO TAX RECORDS

There are two methods for obtaining access to information from the Internal Revenue Service tax records: federal court order, and written request. These methods vary according to the source of the information sought.

Federal Court Order

All accompanying forms and schedules, including employer W-2 forms, and any other information provided either by the taxpayer himself, or one of his representatives, can be obtained only with an order from a Federal District Court under Title 26, US Code, Sec. 6103i(1). Fortunately, the procedure is not particularly difficult. The motion for release of these records is an ex parte (one-sided) proceeding and may be made before a federal magistrate. Additionally, the elements and standard of proof required for release are easily met. The government's required showing is as follows:

° There is reasonable cause to believe that a federal crime has been committed.

° There is reasonable cause to believe that the above described returns and return information are or may be relevant to a matter relating to the commission of this crime. (emphasis added)

° The returns and return information are sought exclusively for use in a federal criminal investigation or proceeding concerning such crime.

° The information sought to be disclosed cannot be reasonably obtained, under the circumstances, from another source.

The key points to note are the authority of a local federal magistrate to order-release the relatively low standard of proof required (that is, mere reasonable cause), and the requirement of the mere possibility that the information sought may be relevant to the crime under investigation. Unlike the administrative subpoena, this procedure does require reasonable cause to believe that a federal offense has been actually committed.

Access to tax records can be important for several reasons. First of all, many people have an ingrained fear of lying to the IRS and will list even illegal income as "miscellaneous." Secondly, tax records now include notices of interest income and can be useful in discovering large cash deposits which have not been placed in noninterest bearing accounts. Tax returns are also useful in locating missing witnesses.

Written Request

Information in a person's IRS tax records, which is not part of his tax returns, or which was not submitted either by the taxpayer himself or his representative, can be obtained with a written request signed by the Secretary of the Army to the Commissioner of the Internal Revenue Service. As a practical matter, such third party information will normally exist only if there has been an independent IRS audit or investigation. For that reason, this method of access will not be generally appropriate. Under current procedures, information falling in this second category will be automatically released for trial counsel obtaining court ordered access to tax information described earlier in this FC.

COURT-ORDERED ACCESS TO GRAND JURY INFORMATION

While it is certainly not routine for the accused pending court-martial to be concurrently investigated by federal grand juries, the increased emphasis by the Justice Department on defense fraud, waste, and abuse merits at least a passing consideration of the techniques for accessing grand jury information set forth in Rule 6(e) of the Federal Rules of Criminal Procedure. The scope of this article limits the treatment of this subject to a brief summary. A more detailed discussion can be found in Wright, Federal Practice and Procedure, sec. 106 (1983).

Release of information obtained by a grand jury requires a court order from the supervising federal district court judge. Such order can be obtained if the government can show in an ex parte motion either that the information sought falls outside the scope of Rule 6(e), or that a judicial proceeding is either pending or in progress and the government has a particularized need for disclosure that outweighs any continuing interest in secrecy.

INFORMATION OUTSIDE RULE 6(e)

Rule 6(e) governing grand jury secrecy extends to "all matters occurring before the grand jury." This definition normally extends to evidence presented before the grand jury and any information indicating the direction of the grand jury proceedings. As a general rule, federal courts have held, however, that documents which have an independent existence from the grand jury proceedings (for example, corporate records, as opposed to testimony transcripts) are not "matters occurring before the grand jury" and therefore do not fall within Rule 6(e). This does not mean, however, that one can bypass the necessity of obtaining a court order to secure the release of these documents. This requirement extends to any information obtained through the grand jury process.

RELEASE OF 6(e) INFORMATION

The government can obtain the release of evidence presented before a grand jury, often referred to as 6(e) information, by establishing in an ex parte motion that failure to disclose this information will result in an injustice at a pending or current judicial proceeding. The existence of a judicial proceeding must be more than merely speculative. Consequently, it would not be possible to obtain grand jury information during the preliminary phase of a case investigation. Accessing this information, however, can be extremely valuable to supplement or further develop the government's case once court-martial charges have been preferred.

A sliding scale type of analysis is used to balance the importance of disclosure against the continued need for secrecy. The commonly noted reasons for grand jury secrecy are as follows:

- To prevent the intimidation of grand jury members and witnesses.

- To prevent the flight from prosecution of grand jury targets.

- To protect the reputations of innocent persons investigated, but later cleared by the grand jury.

These policy considerations supporting secrecy understandably diminish in importance in those cases where federal prosecution has either been completed or declined.

CAVEAT: An assistant US attorney is assigned to every jury to advise them during their investigations and deliberations. He, and such technical experts as he deems necessary, are granted automatic access to grand jury information solely for the purpose of assisting the grand jury. It is not uncommon for Army CID agents to be attached to a US attorney's office for the purpose of assisting in an Army related grand jury investigation. These agents are not at liberty to disclose 6(e) information to trial counsel unless the federal district court has first granted the motion for release described above. Government personnel ignore these restrictions at their risk. Violations of Rule 6(e) are classified as misdemeanors in the Federal Rules of Criminal Procedure. In certain cases, however, some federal circuits have held Rule 6(e) violations to be obstructions of justice, thereby making them felony offenses.

CREDIT REPORTS

Reports maintained by consumer reporting agencies on individuals are defined by the Fair Credit Reporting Act, Title 15, US Code, Sec. 1681, et seq (and the following one). These reports can contain a wealth of information on the personal background and prior financial transactions of a suspect. As a general rule, Section 1681 (b)(1) of this act requires trial counsel to obtain a federal court order prior to gaining access to these reports. There is one important exception to this rule that is extremely useful in locating missing witnesses. Title 15, US Code, Sec. 1681(f) specifically authorizes release to government agencies of a consumer's employment. It is important to note that the protective procedures according to consumer reports by the Fair Credit Reporting Act apply only to individuals and do not restrict access to similar reports on corporations or other business entities.

RIGHT TO FINANCIAL PRIVACY ACT

Trial counsel conducting or advising on financial background investigations must familiarize themselves with the procedural requirements of the Right to Financial Privacy Act, Title 12, US Code, Sec. 3401, et seq, implemented by AR 190-6. This act restricts the government's access to personal financial records maintained by financial institutions. "Person" under the act is defined as an individual or a partnership of five or fewer individuals. "Financial institution" includes banks, savings and loan associations, credit unions, and other consumer financial institutions located within either the continental United States or its territorial possessions.

The act sets forth a general policy that financial institutions should maintain the confidentiality of the personal financial records within its possession and establishes various procedural protections to limit unwarranted access by the government. The act establishes five basic avenues by which the government can obtain release of financial records. These avenues are as follows:

° Customer authorization.

° Administrative subpoena.

° Search warrant.

° Judicial subpoena.

° Formal written request to the financial institution.

Normally, the government is required to notify the person that his records are being sought and to inform him of the purpose of the inquiry, prior to gaining access to the records. The government can gain access to financial institution records covertly, (that is, without notice to the target) only upon successfully showing the appropriate judge or magistrate that one of the following situations exists:

° The investigation being conducted is lawful.

° The records being sought may be relevant to the investigation.

° There is reason to believe that notice to the person will compromise the investigation.

Unless a delay in notification is obtained, the government is obligated by the act not only to notify the subject of its inquiry, but to draft a motion to quash access to the records sought and to send a copy of this motion with instructions for filing to the target. AR 190-6 provides a detailed analysis of the requirements of the Right to Financial Privacy Act and should be reviewed by trial counsel before any financial investigation in initiated. Note that this statute imposes both civil and criminal sanctions against the government and financial institutions. The civil sanctions for violations of this act are particularly severe, as the statute expressly provides for punitive damages.

CONDUCTING FINANCIAL INTERVIEWS

The interview, if properly conducted, can greatly enhance the success of an investigation when monetary interest or greed for wealth was the principal motive of the participants. Lacking the necessary skills, traditional criminal investigators have been reluctant to broaden the scope of their investigations into the financial area. They thereby sacrifice the potential value of leads that might have been successfully developed if properly explored.

Few skills are so important to the economic crime investigator as having a firm command of interviewing techniques. Through interviews the investigator can obtain and develop:

- ° Information that establishes the essential elements of the crime.

- ° Leads for developing cases and gathering other evidence.

- ° The cooperation of victims and witnesses.

- ° Information concerning the personal background and personal economic motives of potential trial witnesses.

Interviewing for financial data involves the systematic questioning of persons who have knowledge of the events, the people involved, and the physical evidence surrounding the case under investigation. Financial interviewing is not unlike the other kinds of interviewing traditional criminal investigators perform. However, in financial interviewing, the evidence often develops in bits and pieces, which, when viewed separately, may appear to lead nowhere. Frustration is common, and tactics and techniques may have to be modified and carefully employed. Diligence, patience, and persistence are essential to successful results. Economic crime investigations often take a long time to complete, require a tremendous amount of leg work, and are often slow to result in arrests.

Interview Planning

Every investigator should follow a set of guidelines to ensure that the primary objectives of the interview are met. The actual approach to and conduct of the interview depend a great deal on the investigator's personality, background, knowledge, and experience. Good planning enables the investigator to get the most out of the interview in the least amount of time. The guidelines that follow list the types of information or expertise relating to the case under investigation. They are presented as a guide only and should be modified as a particular occasion requires.

Planning begins by determining the status and title of the subject or interviewee. Background checks and scrutiny of intelligence files can serve as a starting point. If the interviewee is of reputable stature in the community (for example, a banker, broker, or lawyer), extensive background searches may not be necessary. Usually, however, complete background inquiries are merited and should be undertaken.

Before conducting an interview, the investigator should ascertain as many facts as are reasonably available. This should include a careful review of all relevant documents and reports that have been obtained prior to the interview.

The investigator should keep an open mind and be receptive to all information regardless of its nature, and be prepared to develop the information further. If the investigator is not flexible, a great deal of the time may be wasted in asking unnecessary questions, resulting in a voluminous statement of little or no value. Although the investigator may find it easier to adhere to a fixed pattern of interviewing, or to rely upon a series of questions or topics, rigid adherence to any notes or outline will seriously handicap flexibility. The outline and data should serve only as aids, not as a substitute for original and spontaneous questioning.

Time and Place of Interview

There are very real advantages (principally to the efficiency of the investigation) in conducting the interview at the investigator's office. In some cases, however, it may be far more advisable to visit the witness at his home or office because--

- ° The interviewee is more likely to have papers, appointment books, and the like, available if they become relevant to the interview. The interviewee may also be in a position to immmediately call on family members or coworkers for additional information and corroborative evidence.

COMPREHENSIVE GUIDELINES FOR INFORMATION TO BE COLLECTED IN FINANCIAL INTERVIEWS

Identification

1. Full name
2. Alias
3. Reason for alias

Birth

4. Date
5. Place
6. Citizenship
7. Father's name
8. Living?
9. Mother's name
10. Living?

Address During Pertinent Years

11. Residence
12. Phone number
13. Business
14. Phone number
15. Any other present or prior addresses

Marital Status (helpful in locating undisclosed bank accounts)

16. Present status; if married, date and place of marriage
17. Divorced--when, where
18. Spouse's maiden name
19. Spouse's parents living?
20. Children's names and ages--dependents?

Occupation

21. Present position
22. Company name and address
23. Present salary
24. Length of time employed
25. Any part-time or additional employment
26. Prior occupations
27. Spouse's occupation

General Background

28. Physical health
29. Mental health
30. Education
31. Military service
32. Social Security number (for identification purposes)
33. Ever been arrested?
34. Ever been bankrupt?

Financial Institutions, Business and Personal

35. Checking accounts
36. Savings accounts
37. Safe deposits boxes (request inventory of safe deposit boxes)
38. In whose name
39. Contents
    a. Generally
    b. Largest amount of cash? When held?
40. Contents at last visit
41. Does anyone else have access?
42. Trusts: beneficiary, donor, or trustee
43. Credit union
44. Brokers
45. Currency exchanges used
46. Cashier's checks
47. Money orders, bank drafts, travelers' checks

Sources of Income

48. Salaries, wages, business receipts
49. Interest and dividends
50. Sale of securities
51. Rents and royalties
52. Pensions, trusts, annuities, etc.
53. Gifts (money, property, etc.)
54. Inheritances
55. Loans
56. Mortgages
57. Sale of assets

COMPREHENSIVE GUIDELINES FOR INFORMATION TO BE COLLECTED IN FINANCIAL INTERVIEWS (CONT)

Sources of Income (Cont)

58. Municipal bond interest
59. Insurance settlements
60. Damages from legal actions
61. Any other source of funds, ever

Net Income and Expenditures

62. Current cash on hand, including cash in safe deposit boxes, but not including cash in bank accounts
63. Location of current cash
64. Largest amount of cash ever on hand, location
65. End-of-year cash balances
66. Notes receivable
67. Mortgages receivable
68. Life insurance policies
69. Automobiles
70. Real estate
71. Stocks, bonds, and other securities
72. Jewelry, furs
73. Airplanes, boats
74. Any other assets valued over $500

Liabilities

75. Payables
76. Loans
77. Assets purchased by financing
78. Mortgages

Expenditures

79. Debt reduction
80. Insurance premiums
81. Interest expense
82. Contributions
83. Medical
84. Travel
85. Real estate and other taxes
86. Servants' wages
87. Casualty losses

Business Operation

88. Name and address
89. Date organized and nature (corporation, partnership, or whatever)
90. Title and duties
91. Investment, where and when
92. Associates

Books and Records

93. Accounting system, cash or accrual
94. Period covered
95. Location
96. Name of person maintaining and controlling
97. Types: journals, ledgers, minute books, cancelled checks, bank statements, invoices, cash register tapes, appointment books
98. Name of outside auditor

Business Receipts

99. Form: checks or cash
100. Are all receipts deposited? Where?
101. Are business receipts segregated from personal ones?
102. Are expenses ever paid with undeposited receipts?
103. Cash checks for customers?
104. Checks to cash or other withdrawals

- It may be more convenient for the interviewee, thus making it more likely that he or she will agree to the meeting for the interview.

- There may be fewer interruptions and distractions than at the investigator's office, where inquiries from supervisors and colleagues are common.

- It also may be advantageous to catch the potential interviewee off guard, before he or she can have second thoughts, talk to someone else, develop fear, or be contacted by the subjects of the investigation.

When the interview is to be held away from the investigator's office, a specific appointment should be made unless there is a logical reason not to do so, such as catching the witness off guard.

Interviews should always be arranged so that there is enough time to conduct a full interview. It is always better to have extra time than to create additional irritations by terminating an interivew early or making excuses for breaking or delaying appointments which are scheduled to follow. When the investigator is going to be late, he should telephone, apologize, and inform the person to be interviewed when he will arrive, or schedule another appointment immediately. If an interview is attempted without a prior appointment, the investigator may find the person to be completely unprepared. This problem is particularly important when the investigator wants to obtain documents, such as canceled checks of a victim, sales literature from a witness, or advice and supporting documents from an expert. It is advisable to tell the interviewee what information will be needed at the time of the interview. When calling on a person without an appointment, it is important to select a time that would be least likely to irritate the interviewee. Although this seems like an elementary point, investigators who just "drop in" take the chance of irritating the interviewee--a situation that may undermine the interview's success.

The investigator should take the interviewee's special characteristics into account. If the investigator finds that the witness or victim speaks a language he is unfamiliar with, appointments must be made by other office personnel who can speak the language. The investigator should make special plans to be certain there is no misunderstanding as to time and place and should arrange for someone fluent in the foreign language to go along.

The process of making the appointment could itself be a source of valuable information. The response of a witness or victim to the request for the interview may alert the investigator to special problems that might be encountered (such as language problems, fear, lack of awareness on the part of the witness that he or she was a victim), which will help him to plan the forthcoming interview properly.

Setting

When the setting for the interview is under the investigator's control, a place should be selected to provide a minimum number of obstacles to talking and, more important, to listening. If the interview must be conducted at the enforcement agency, a room that ensures privacy should be used. It is important that the room be free of decorative distractions, yet pleasant and equipped with comfortable chairs. Distractions, such as telephone noises, other voices, or other conversations can have a disastrous effect on the recall capabilities of a victim or witness. In addition, interruptions from telephone calls or other persons convey to the interviewee that the investigator is not really interested in what is being said.

An investigator who is interested in obtaining as much information as possible should also consider other possibilities for creating an environment that will put a witness at ease and heighten the witness's trust in him. For example, the interviewee should be encouraged to tell the story in his or her own way, even if it rambles. Interruptions should be limited to clarification of the interviewee's statement.

Investigator's Demeanor

When dealing with any member of the public, whether in person or on the telephone, the investigator must always be efficient, courteous, polite, and careful. The investigator represents his agency, and the impression he gives is the impression the public will have of the agency.

The following are some suggestions for an investigator's conduct during an interview:

° The investigator should avoid talking down to the person being interviewed. Hints of disrespect or condescension can quickly turn a cooperative subject into an uncooperative one.

° Language that disparages the intelligence or competence of the interviewee should be avoided, even if it is quite evident that the person acted foolishly in being victimized, in not preventing victimization of a friend or associate, or in failing to notify the enforcement agency when it would have been common sense to do so.

° The investigator should be sensitive to the personal concerns of the victim or witness, especially when these involve perceptions of how the interviewee may be treated because of sex, race, religion, or ethnic background.

° A businesslike demeanor is essential. The interview must be conducted in a professional manner. Certain pleasantries are sometimes necessary, but the interview should not become a social occasion.

- The investigator should avoid an authoritarian attitude and should not attempt to dominate the interview.

- The investigator should make it clear that anyone, no matter how smart or well trained, may be victimized, and that others have had similar experiences.

- A sympathetic and respectful attitude is essential. Never suggest that a victim is a victim because of something he did. The investigator must be extremely careful not to injure the victim's pride in his or her own judgment, not to belittle the loss, and not to build up any false hopes as to the possibilities of recouping all or part of the loss.

- Careful thought should be given to the language that is employed during the interview to make sure that it is consistent with the approach and understandable to the interviewee. Of particular importance is avoidance of bureaucratic jargon.

- The investigator should compliment the victim or complaining witness for taking the trouble to cooperate or complain, explaining that not to do so would be playing into the hands of the subject of the investigation.

- Lastly, every interview should be concluded with a statement of sincere appreciation. This encourages the subject to maintain contact if he or she recalls more information.

Basic Questions

The interviewee should completely answer the following basic questions:

- Who? All persons referred to should be completely identified. This includes the following information: description, address, alias, "trading as," "also known as," citizenship, reputation, and associates. If the person cannot be named, a physical description should be requested. The description should include age; height; weight; color of eyes, hair, and skin; description of build; clothing; unusual markings, scars; and mental or physical defects. Questions also should cover any aids worn by the individual, such as glasses, hearing aids, wig or toupee, cane, braces, and other items.

- What? Complete details of what happened. Trace the events from beginning to end. Every detail should be determined.

- Where? Complete details regarding locations where all events took place. A description of the location should include the general area, as well as the identification of the person or people having control.

- When? The time may be established by direct questioning, by relating the incident to some known event, or by associating the event with some person, place, or thing.

- Why? Everything is done for a reason. Determine the motive by questioning the witnesses about their actions. What caused them to act? Who caused them to act? Why did they act as they did? Because these are the most important questions, especially when relating to or reflecting criminal purpose, they should receive special consideration.

Other Considerations

The economic crime investigator often faces problems and obstacles related to certain characteristics of personal situations of victims or witnesses. There may also be different problems with interviewees who are victims than with those who are only witnesses.

A witness who is not a victim may be uncooperative for a variety of reasons, such as fear of reprisal, dislike of law enforcement, or fear or self-incrimination. Even totally innocent witnesses may consider it just too much trouble to spend their time assisting a law enforcement investigator.

Technical experts may be reluctant to participate at the outset of an investigation for fear of inviting a civil liability suit. For example, an honest certified public accountant who prepared the financial statements for a business that was defrauded might be concerned about being sued for negligence because the fraud was not uncovered in the course of performing the professional work.

Both privately owned and government enterprises operate on the basis of public trust and confidence. Banks, savings and loan associations, business organizations in general, brokerage houses, fiduciary organizations, and government agencies rely in large part on public confidence for their success. Not only may commission of an economic crime cause an immediate financial loss, but the attendant publicity may also cause a loss in public confidence and a corresponding drop in business prestige or public trust. The enterprise may prefer to conceal the crime and forego a prosecution rather than risk a loss of public confidence.

As a result of the personal embarassment felt by victims, the investigator often has difficulty in both locating victims and getting them to participate in an interview or on a witness stand. Most victims do not welcome appearances in court, particularly when they know there is nothing to gain or little chance that it will help to restore their loss.

Also to be considered is the emotional state of victims or witnesses being interviewed. The loss of all or part of their money has been a shock if they are victims; nonvictims may have great apprehensions about being involved.

Victims will often have unsupported opinions regarding the circumstances connected with the crime. These should not be disparaged, but should be pursued to a logical conclusion.

RECORDING INFORMATION OBTAINED FROM INTERVIEWS

The principal purpose of an interview is to obtain all the facts helpful in resolving the case. This places a responsibility on investigators to maintain the evidence they collect; therefore, it is necessary to prepare a permanent record of every interview. A listing of guidelines for information that should become part of the permanent record (report) of every interview follows. These guidelines may have to be altered to meet the specific occasion.

GUIDELINES FOR INFORMATION TO BE RECORDED IN INTERVIEWS

About the Interview

- Location, date, and time.
- Name of investigators.

About the Subjects Being Investigated

- Names of promoters, their representatives, agents, and the like (individuals, and company names).
- Addresses of individuals and companies.
- Legal status of companies (corporations, partnerships, state of incorporation, and the like).
- Telephone numbers of individuals and companies.
- Physical descriptions.
- Title, salary, tenure, duties, and responsiblities of suspect (particularly important in embezzlement cases).

About Contact Between Subjects and Witnesses

- How was initial contact made?
  - Advertisement in newspaper, radio, or television? Get name of paper or station and dates.
  - Sales letter? Get copies of letter, envelopes, and any other material enclosed with letter.

- Personal contact? By telephone or in person? Get dates, names, locations, and content of conversations.

- References through third party (attorney, friend, or whoever)?

° Were there any previous relationships between promoter and victim?

° How did the promoters or their representatives get the victim's name or learn about the victim?

About the Situation and Content of Meetings, Conversations, Transactions

° Date, location, and time of occurrence.

° Names, addresses, titles, and the like, of all who were present.

° Full details of all representations (promises).

- Method of representation.

- What was said?

- What was shown? What was handed out (letters, brochures, prospectuses, sales literature, warranties, guarantees, contracts, and the like)?

- Which person made each representation?

° Victim's degree of reliance on representation.

- Did victim have any mental reservations?

- Did he or she express them?

- Did he or she ask any questions?

- What were the answers? Who made them?

- How were his or her mental reservations overcome? By whom?

- Was anything done to discourage victim from a detailed reading of papers, or from consulting friends, attorneys, accountant, banker, or anyone else in particular?

° Representations that victim believes were false.

° Representations that victim believes were omitted but should have been told.

- ° Was victim put under any time or other severe pressure to enter into transaction? How?

- ° Full details of transaction.

    - Amount of dollars.

    - Method of payment--check, cash, agreements or contracts to pay in future, or whatever.

    - Date and circumstances of payment--in person, by mail, to whom, and the like.

About the Victim

- ° Name, address, telephone numbers (home and business).

- ° Motivation behind the complaint.

    - To recover losses (Note: Circumstances will dictate when the investigator should advise victim that criminal action does not guarantee restitution or ensure success in a civil action, but it is proper to point out that one possible outcome of action is restitution following criminal or government civil action.)

    - Anger or outrage.

    - To protect others from same scheme.

- ° If information as to victim's motivation is not based on victim's statement, what is the basis for above information?

- ° Victim's background (may assist in finding out how promoter got victim's name and thus help in locating other victims).

- ° How and when victim discovered representations were false.

- ° Has victim complained to promoter?

    - What did victim do or say?

    - Did victim complain himself or herself, or through a friend or attorney?

    - Has victim complained to any other private or public agency? With what results?

- ° Financial losses suffered.

- ° Victim's source of funds lost.

° Psychological suffering.

° Has victim withheld information from members of his or her family or business associates?

° Victim's willingness to assist in investigation and testify in court (Note: Circumstances will dictate appropriate timing for addressing these issues; for example, this may not be suitable in the early stages of interviewing noncomplaining witnesses.)

° Will victim sign statement or affidavit swearing to truth of what was said?

About Physical Evidence

° Obtain, borrow, or copy all physical evidence--cancelled checks, receipts, brochures, sales literature, prospectuses, warranties, guarantees, letters, envelopes, contracts, and the like.

° Give receipt for all items borrowed.

° Have interviewee initial and date each page of each item.

DIRECT METHODS OF TRACING FINANCIAL TRANSACTIONS

SOURCES OF FINANCIAL INFORMATION--BANKS

It would be impractical for all economic crime investigators to master the art of following internal banking audit trails in order to obtain evidence of financial transactions pertinent to a particular criminal investigation. Because of ongoing improvements in electronic data-processing systems, bank recordkeeping systems are far too complex and change too rapidly to warrant training of economic crime investigators in this area. It is vital, however, for investigators to acquire and maintain a high degree of familiarity with the capability and responsibility of banks to maintain and retrieve, upon appropriate request, key information concerning financial transactions with their customers.

Investigators should recognize the fact that, in most instances, bank records are not readily obtainable. Substantial legal requirements must usually be met to justify legal process (subpoena, search warrant, and the like), which banks customarily will demand as a condition for disclosure.

Thus, preliminary investigation to lay the basis for obtaining such records is of the utmost importance.

The availability of the investigative avenues often determines whether a promising investigation will grind to a halt or proceed successfully. Legal advise from a prosecutor or agency legal counsel should be sought in all such instances. However, it should also be recognized that bank officials and employees can be questioned by investigators in the same way as any other potential witnesses and that their responses to proper inquiries may provide important information worth further pursuit or nonrecord information as to movements, relationships, and even transactions in which the subject of the investigation may be engaged.

The following information can be of inestimable value to economic crime investigators in seeking information from banks concerning pertinent financial transactions of economic crime perpetrators. It is based, in part, on the Operational Guidelines issued by the American Bankers Association to all member banks in the United States and on the Training Guides issued by the US Department of the Treasury.

Types of Banks

Banks are classified primarily by their major services:

- Commerical banks offer businesses and individuals such services as checking accounts, loans, and exchange instruments.

- Savings banks and savings and loan associations handle savings accounts and mortgage loans.

- Trust companies handle property for others under various types of fiduciary accomodations.

Many banks combine all three services.

Banks are organized under either state or national banking laws.

The basic bank functions are as follows:

- Receive deposits.

- Pay checks.

- Transfer funds.

- Make loans.

- Collect sundry financial instruments.

- ° Hold and administer property for others.

- ° Perform other services, such as safe deposit box rentals.

Importance of Bank Records

Bank records are perhaps the single most important financial source available to an economic crime investigator. In addition to their use as evidence to prove a criminal violation, a bank's records may provide leads on sources of funds, expenditures, and personal affairs.

Internal Bookkeeping Procedures

The internal banking recordkeeping practices and procedures are not only complex but are constantly changing because of the growing sophistication of computer technology. The nation's banks are moving steadily toward an electronic funds transfer system, which will eliminate the use of checks. Such a system will automatically transfer money from the account of the purchaser to the account of the seller. The "paper trails" will disappear.

Detailed familiarity with the intricacies of internal bank operations is not essential to the investigator in order to obtain the types of information necessary for investigations. What is essential is the knowledge that records of customers' transactions are maintained and retained.

Retention of Records

The provisions of Titles I and II of Public Law 91-508, Finanical Recordkeeping and Currency and Foreign Transactions Act, make it mandatory to retain records of customers' transactions.

US Treasury Regulations, implementing Public Law 91-508, provide in part that an original, microfilm, or other copy or reproduction of most demand deposits (checking account) and savings account records must be retained for 5 years. The records must include--

- ° Signature cards.

- ° Statements, ledger cards, or other records disclosing all transactions, that is, deposits and withdrawals.

- ° Copies of customers' checks, bank drafts, money orders, and cashier's checks drawn on the bank or issued and payable by it.

In addition, banks must retain for a 2-year period all records necessary to--

- ° Reconstruct a customer's checking account (the records must include copies of the customer's deposit tickets).

° Trace and supply a description of a check deposited to a customer's checking account.

All of the above requirements apply to checks written or deposits made in excess of $100. It should be noted that most banks find it cheaper to microfilm all pertinent records, including the checks and deposits in amounts less than $100, rather than sort their records into two categories. Therefore, if a particular transaction is less than $100 and appears to be of particular interest, there is a strong likelihood that the necessary records to identify the transaction are available.

The regulations further provide that, whatever system banks use to photocopy or microfilm checks, drafts, or money orders, both sides must be reproduced unless the reverse side is blank.

The regulations also provide that banks maintain their records in such a manner that they can be made available, upon request, within a "reasonable period of time."

BANK RECORDS

The bank records identified and discussed below are limited to those of particular interest to economic crime investigators.

Signature Cards

The signature card is the evidence of a contract between the customer and bank.

When a depositor opens an account, the bank requires that a signature card be signed. By signing the card the depositor becomes a party to a contract with the bank under which he accepts all rules and regulations of the bank and authorizes the bank to honor orders for withdrawing funds. For a corporation or a partnerhsip account, the signature card is accompanied by copies of resolutions of the board of directors or partnership agreements naming the person authorized to draw checks on the accounts.

The signature card is a source of valuable information. Although its form varies, the card usually contains such data as banking connections, the date and amount of the initial deposit, and so on. The initial deposit traced through the bank's records may disclose a source of income. The identification of the official who opened the account might be significant, especially if the depositor used an alias.

Many banks investigate the banking references given by the new customer. They may also make inquiries of various credit-reporting agencies. This information is contained in a correspondence file or a credit file, which may contain comments of the official who opened the account showing information given by the depositor when opening the account.

In banks using ADP (Automatic Data Processing), the signature card also contains an account number assigned to the customer. In tracing information about a subject's transactions with the bank, the account number must be used. If it does not appear on the signature card, it can be located in the bank's cross-reference file. These assigned account numbers are encoded on other documents relating to the depositor by means of a system called MICR (Magnetic Ink Character Recognition). The card may also contain the depositor's Social Security Number.

The signature card may define the account as either a regular or a special checking account. The main difference between the two accounts is the service charges made by the bank. The regular checking account is used mostly by businesses and individuals who maintain large average balances. The special checking account is used by individuals who usually have small account balances.

When requesting the signature card, the investigator should check whether the bank maintains any type of central file. Most large banks maintain some type of central file that lists all the bank's departments with which a customer has had dealings. If the bank has such a file, the investigator does not need to check with each department to obtain complete information.

It is important to remember that the subject may at one time have had a bank account that was later closed. Requests for information from a bank about a subject should always include a reference to both active and closed accounts. Usually records of closed accounts are maintained in a separate file.

Negotiated Checks

Cancelled checks written by a subject or received from others provide the economic crime investigator with much more than amounts, payees, and endorsees.

° Recognizing "cashed" checks.
  Of particular interest to the investigator are checks that have been cashed. All banks use a series of codes or symbols, which they usually imprint on the front of a check, to show that the check has been "cashed." An example of "cashed codes" used by banks is shown on page 34. The specific codes used by your particular area can be obtained locally.

° Tracing checks.
  Tracing checks is facilitated by the use of bank identification symbols. As stated earlier, investigators do not have to understand the internal bookkeeping procedures used by banks. However, the concept of bank identification symbols should be of interest. All checks printed for banking institutions contain an ABA transit number (see example on page 35). These numbers represent an identification code developed by the American Bankers Association. The ABA transit number allows for the routing of a check back to the bank of origin.

In the process of routing, a trail is left that enables the tracing of each specific item. (A complete listing of the ABA Numerical System Identification Code follows the ABA Transit Number diagram).

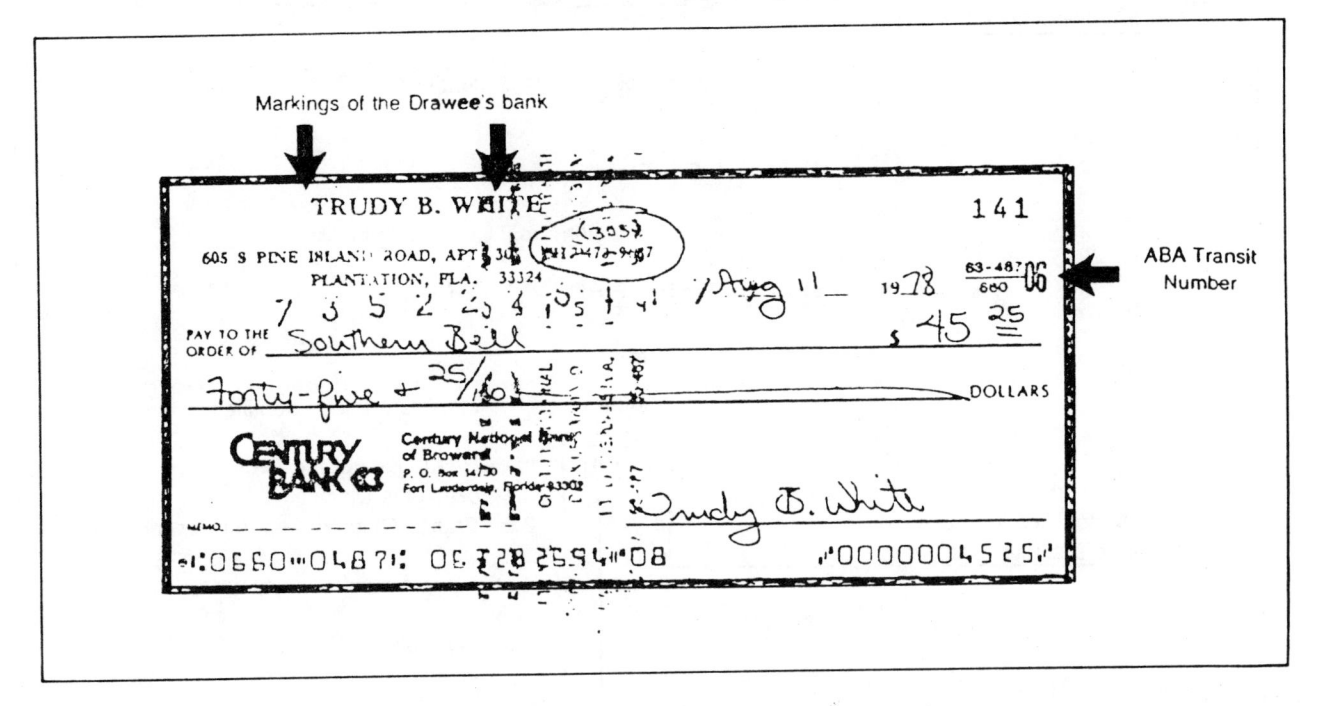

Checked Cash Codes

° MICR (Magnetic Ink Character Recognition).
  MICR is a machine language and is a standard in check design to which all banks must conform. Numeric information is printed in magnetic ink on the bottom of bank checks and other documents. This coding is electronically scanned by computers, which convert the magnetic ink notations into electronic impulses intelligible to a computer. MICR information is printed in groupings called fields (see example following the list of Routing Symbols). On bank checks, the first field on the left is the Federal Reserve check-routing code and the next is the ABA transit number. These numbers also appear in the upper right corner of the check. The account number field shows the drawer's assigned account number at the bank. When the check is processed through the bank an additional field is added on the right for the amount of the check. The dollar amount of the check should always equal the encoded MICR amount. These two figures should be compared to be sure the subject did not alter the returned check. All checks, drafts, and similar items that are not encoded with magnetic ink cannot be cleared through the Federal Reserve system without special handling and delay.

AMERICAN BANKERS ASSOCIATION CODE

No. 1-49 identifies the city

No. 50-99 identifies the state

| 68 | 424 |

514

This number identifies the bank

Thus the number 68-424 is identified as follows:

68 - State of Virginia

424 - Arlington Trust Co., Arlington, Virginia

FEDERAL RESERVE ROUTING CODE

(1)

68-424

| 5 | 1 | 4 |

(1) This number identifies:

- 1 - Head office of the Federal Reserve District
- 2-5 - Branch Office of Federal Reserve Dist.

This number signifies:

- 0 - Available for Immediate Credit

Deferred Credit

1-5

Designates the state in which the drawee bank is located

- 6-9 - Special collection arrangements

No. 1-9 identifies the Federal Reserve Districts

Thus the number 514 is identified as follows:

5 - Fifth Federal Reserve District

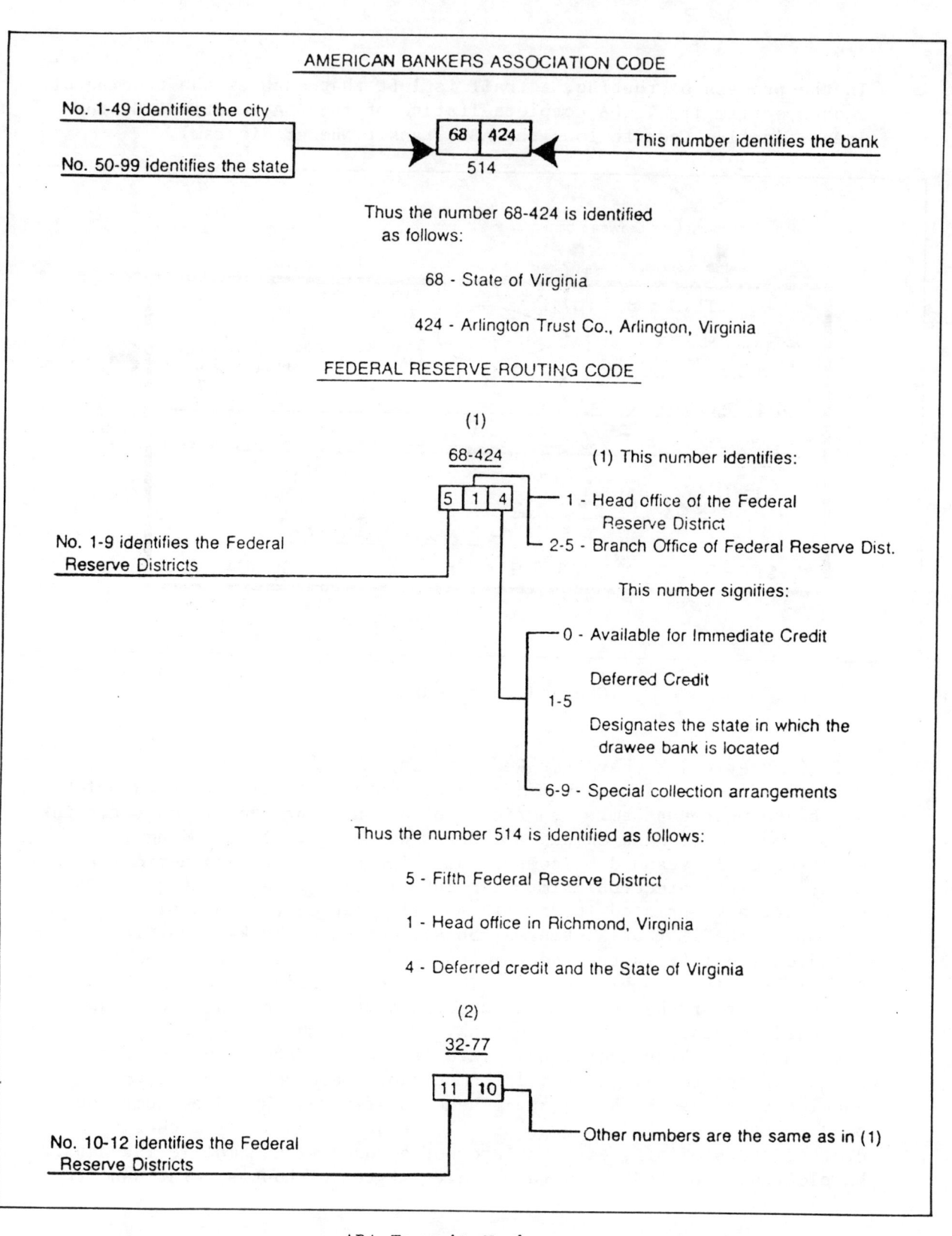

1 - Head office in Richmond, Virginia

4 - Deferred credit and the State of Virginia

(2)

32-77

| 11 | 10 |

Other numbers are the same as in (1)

No. 10-12 identifies the Federal Reserve Districts

ABA Transit Number

34

Index to Prefix Numbers of Cities and States

Numbers 1 to 49 inclusive are Prefixes for Cities
Numbers 50 to 99 inclusive are Prefixes for States

Prefix Numbers 50 to 58 are Eastern States
Prefix Number 59 is Alaska, American Samoa, Guam, Hawaii, Puerto Rico and Virgin Islands
Prefix Numbers 60 to 69 are Southeastern States
Prefix Numbers 70 to 79 are Central States
Prefix Numbers 80 to 88 are Southwestern States
Prefix Numbers 90 to 99 are Western States

Prefix Numbers of Cities in Numerical Order

1	New York, NY	18	Kansas City, Mo.	34	Tacoma, Wash.
2	Chicago, Ill.	19	Seattle, Wash.	35	Houston, Texas
3	Philadelphia, Pa.	20	Indianapolis, Ind.	36	St. Joseph, Mo.
4	St. Louis, Mo.	21	Louisville, Ky.	37	Fort Worth, Texas
5	Boston, Mass.	22	St. Paul, Minn.	38	Savannah, Ga.
6	Cleveland, Ohio	23	Denver, Colo.	39	Oklahoma City, Okla.
7	Baltimore, Md.	24	Portland, Ore.	40	Wichita, Kansas
8	Pittsburgh, Pa.	25	Columbus, Ohio	41	Sioux City, Iowa
9	Detroit, Mich.	26	Memphis, Tenn.	42	Pueblo, Colo.
10	Buffalo, NY	27	Omaha, Neb.	43	Lincoln, Neb.
11	San Francisco, Ca.	28	Spokane, Wash.	44	Topeka, Kansas
12	Milwaukee, Wis.	29	Albany, NY	45	Dubuque, Iowa
13	Cincinnati, Ohio	30	San Antonio, Texas	46	Galveston, Texas
14	New Orleans, La.	31	Salt Lake City, Utah	47	Cedar Rapids, Iowa
15	Washington, D. C.	32	Dallas, Texas	48	Waco, Texas
16	Los Angeles, Ca.	33	Des Moines, Iowa	49	Muskogee, Okla.
17	Minneapolis, Minn.				

Prefix Numbers of States in Numerical Order

50	New York	65	Maryland	83	Kansas
51	Connecticut	66	North Carolina	84	Louisiana
52	Maine	67	South Carolina	85	Mississippi
53	Massachusetts	68	Virginia	86	Oklahoma
54	New Hampshire	69	West Virginia	87	Tennessee
55	New Jersey	70	Illinois	88	Texas
56	Ohio	71	Indiana	89	——
57	Rhode Island	72	Iowa	90	California
58	Vermont	73	Kentucky	91	Arizona
59	Alaska, American Samoa, Guam, Hawaii, Puerto Rico, and Virgin Islands	74	Michigan	92	Idaho
		75	Minnesota	93	Montana
		76	Nebraska	94	Nevada
		77	North Dakota	95	New Mexico
60	Pennsylvania	78	South Dakota	96	Oregon
61	Alabama	79	Wisconsin	97	Utah
62	Delaware	80	Missouri	98	Washington
63	Florida	81	Arkansas	99	Wyoming
64	Georgia	82	Colorado		

Numerical System of the American Bankers Association

All banks in an area served by a Federal Reserve bank or branch carry the routing symbol of the Federal Reserve bank or branch.

FEDERAL RESERVE BANKS AND BRANCHES

1. Federal Reserve Bank of Boston Head Office	5-1 / 110	
2. Federal Reserve Bank of New York Head Office	1-120 / 210	
Buffalo Branch	10-26 / 220	
3. Federal Reserve Bank of Philadelphia Head Office	3-4 / 310	
4. Federal Reserve Bank of Cleveland Head Office	0-1 / 410	
Cincinnati Branch	13-43 / 420	
Pittsburgh Branch	8-30 / 430	
5. Federal Reserve Bank of Richmond Head Office	68-3 / 510	
Baltimore Branch	7-27 / 520	
Charlotte Branch	66-20 / 530	
6. Federal Reserve Bank of Atlanta Head Office	64-14 / 610	
Birmingham Branch	61-19 / 620	
Jacksonville Branch	63-19 / 630	
Nashville Branch	87-10 / 640	
New Orleans Branch	14-21 / 650	
7. Federal Reserve Bank of Chicago Head Office	2-30 / 710	
Detroit Branch	9-29 / 720	
8. Federal Reserve Bank of St. Louis Head Office	4-4 / 810	
Little Rock Branch	81-13 / 820	
Louisville Branch	21-59 / 830	
Memphis Branch	26-3 / 840	
9. Federal Reserve Bank of Minneapolis Head Office	17-8 / 910	
Helena Branch	93-26 / 920	
10. Federal Reserve Bank of Kansas City Head Office	18-4 / 1010	
Denver Branch	23-19 / 1020	
Oklahoma City Branch	39-24 / 1030	
Omaha Branch	27-12 / 1040	
11. Federal Reserve Bank of Dallas Head Office	32-3 / 1110	
El Paso Branch	88-1 / 1120	
Houston Branch	35-4 / 1130	
San Antonio Branch	30-72 / 1140	
12. Federal Reserve Bank of San Francisco Head Office	11-37 / 1210	
Los Angeles Branch	16-16 / 1220	
Portland Branch	24-1 / 1230	
Salt Lake City Branch	31-31 / 1240	
Seattle Branch	19-1 / 1250	

Routing Symbols of Banks That Are Members of the Federal Reserve System

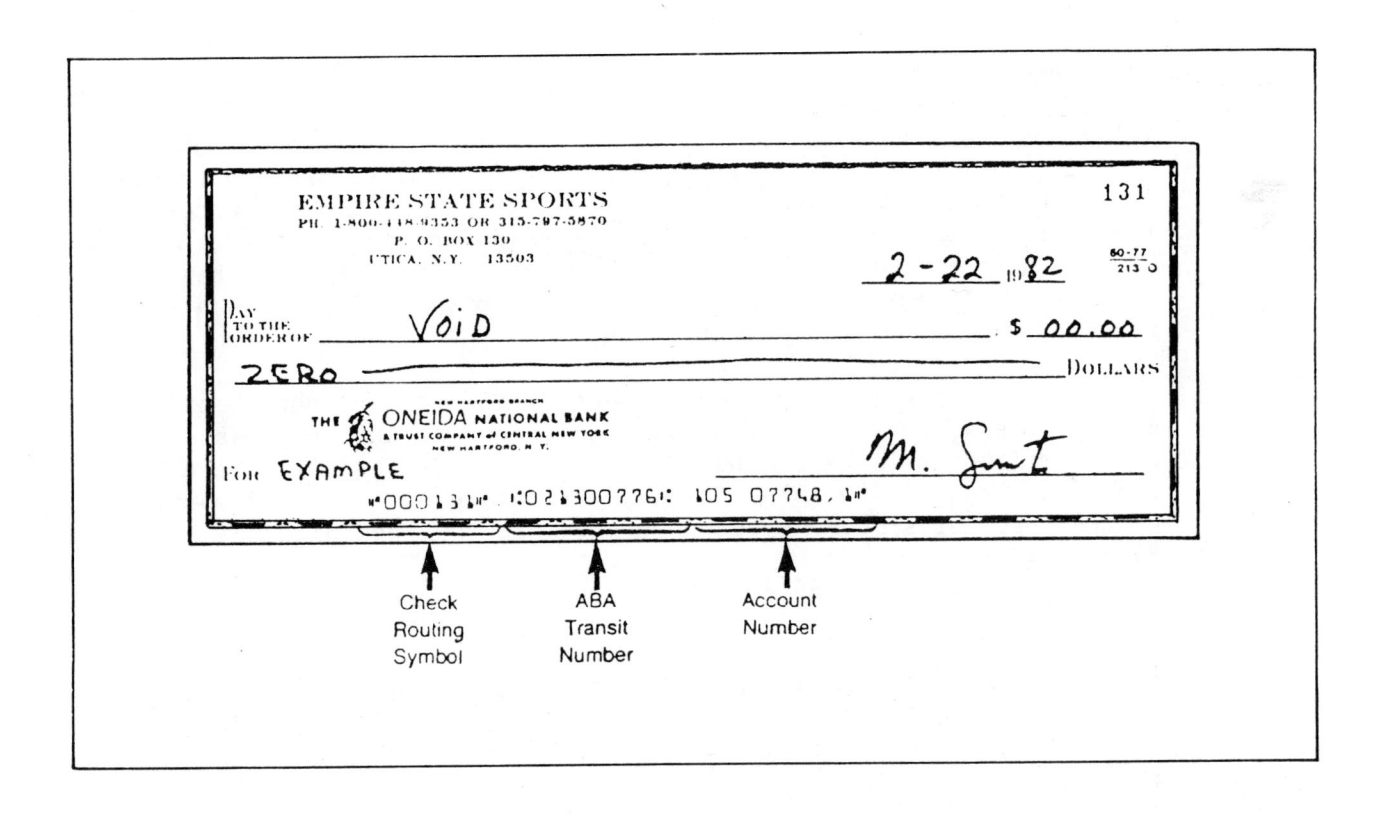

Fields (MICR Information)

° Deposit tickets.
The deposit ticket is the principal source document for crediting the customer's account. Deposits are first recorded on the deposit ticket or slip which usually segregates currency, coins, and checks. The checks are listed separately. In many localities the depositor writes the ABA number or the name of the maker of the check on the deposit ticket. Either of these may help to identify the source of the check. In other localities the bank writes the ABA number on the deposit ticket, and in some banks no identifying data is entered on the deposit ticket. Regardless of the detail contained on a deposit ticket, bank recordkeeping systems are such that items of deposit can be identified and traced to their sources. Unfortunately, the records that enable this tracing may be retained only 1 to 2 years.

In working with deposit tickets, it is important for the economic crime investigator to remember that sometimes the depositor "splits" the deposit, that is, only part of the checks presented are actually deposited. In these instances, the customer either receives cash or requests that part of the proceeds be applied to a note of interest due the bank. In some instances it may be important to determine the total amount of cash and checks presented for deposit before deductions. When this is the case, the investigator should inquire from the bank how split deposits are handled.

° Credit memorandums.

- Telegraphic transfers: On a customer's instructions, funds may be transferred from one bank account to another by wire or telephone. Although the transfer shows as a deposit to the customer's account by means of a credit memo, the detailed records of transfers are usually kept in a special file. If the subject of an investigation has accounts with banks in several cities, the possibility of obtaining funds by wire should be investigated.

- Intrabank transfers: Other departments within a bank can credit the depositor's account for funds collected, such as the proceeds of loans or items held by the bank for collection. It should be noted that items held by the bank for collection are not always deposited to the customer's account but sometimes are remitted directly to the customer.

° Time deposits.

- Savings accounts: These are referred to as time deposits because they are not as readily available to the customer as deposits to a checking account. Funds in a savings account may be subject to a 30-day notice of withdrawal.

- Certificates of deposit (CDs): CDs are funds left with a bank for a definite period of time, for example, 2 years, which draw a higher rate of interest than the ordinary savings account. When these are cashed early, Federal Reserve regulations require a reason.

BANK LEDGERS AND BANK STATEMENTS

Each bank has a bookkeeping department that maintains customer accounts. The basic processes performed in the bookkeeping department are sorting checks to prepare them for posting; posting checks to customers' accounts; posting deposits and other credits; taking care of special items, such as "stop payments"; and proving and balancing general ledger totals for various types of accounts.

The manner in which this work is performed depends on whether a manual or a computerized system is used. Accordingly, different types of records are generated by the two systems. However, a customer's account can be reconstructed under either system.

Bank Ledger Cards--Manual System

Ledger cards are the basic records produced by any manual system. They show all checks, deposits, and other transactions affecting customers' accounts. Ledger cards are the customers' monthly statements. The bank keeps the ledger cards and second, or duplicate, copies of the customers' statements.

Some banks microfilm both these records and the checks returned to the depositors with the monthly statements.

Bank Statements--Computerized System

In an automated system, no historical ledger cards are produced. This is the fundamental difference from bookkeeping records produced under a manual system. However, in a computerized system, statements are produced periodically (generally monthly) for checking accounts. The bank has either microfilm or duplicates of all statements.

It is easier to trace transactions and records with detailed statements, which show all transactions. When only summary, or bobtail, statements are available, all the transactions making up the statement must be reconstructed.

Savings Account Statement

Under the manual system, most banks use ledger cards similar to those for checking accounts to maintain records of savings accounts. A few banks use a system in which statements are mailed to depositors at stated intervals.

In a computerized system the procedure for reconstructing a savings account is similar to that used for checking accounts. In some instances, copies of periodic statements are available to expedite the process. If not, the account must be reconstructed item by item.

EXCHANGE INSTRUMENTS

Exchange instruments are vehicles by which the bank transfers funds. They are cashier's checks, bank drafts, traveler's checks, bank money orders, and certified checks.

Cashier's Checks

These checks issued by the bank are also called treasurer's checks when issued by a trust company. They are frequently an excellent lead to other bank accounts, stock, real property, and other assets. Because they can be held indefinitely, subjects sometimes purchase cashier's checks instead of keeping large amounts of currency. In reconstructing a subject's transactions with cashier's checks, be sure that all checks are accounted for because subjects sometimes exchange previously purchased checks for new ones.

Bank Drafts

These are checks drawn by the issuing bank on its account with another bank. Often this account is in the area where the purchaser desires to make a payment. Bank drafts may also be used when a subject does not want to carry a large amount of cash.

Traveler's Checks

These are checks issued in predetermined amounts by the American Express Company and several large US banks. Local banks purchase them from issuing companies of US banks and then sell them to the public. Traveler's checks require two signatures of the purchaser; one when purchased and the other when cashed.

All accounting for and tracing of traveler's checks is done by serial number. Usually the issuing company keeps records of traveler's checks sent to them by the selling bank.

The local bank that sold the checks may keep a copy of the sales order from which the serial numbers can be obtained. If the numbers are not available, the issuing bank may be able to supply the information if the date the checks were purchased is known. The canceled checks may be obtained from the American Express Company or other issuing banks.

A subject may purchase large amounts of traveler's checks from one bank and deposit them in another to avoid arousing suspicion by having the deposit ticket reflect cash.

Bank Money Orders

These are similar to cashier's checks but are usually for small amounts. Many banks use money orders for small amounts and cashier's checks for larger amounts. Like cashier's checks, money orders may be used by subjects who do not want to use cash.

Certified Checks

These are customer's checks on which "certified" is written or stamped across the front of the checks by the bank. This certification is a guarantee that the bank will pay the checks. Certified checks are liabilities of the bank and, when paid, are kept by the bank. These checks are immediately charged against the customer's account by means of debit memorandums with their bank statements. Some banks permit customers to obtain the original checks by surrendering the debit memorandum.

Bank exchange instruments are often purchased with currency; therefore, they may be good sources of information about a subject's currency transactions.

LOANS

This function of a bank is an important source of information regarding a subject. In keeping records of the loans, the collateral that secures them, and the results of (bank) credit investigations, a bank has a wealth of information that can prove to be very important to an investigation of a subject's affairs.

When a bank makes a commerical loan to an individual, it requires a detailed statement of the assets and liabilities of the borrower. The loan file also includes the results of credit inquiries showing paying habits, amounts of loans, and present unpaid balances.

A bank credit department maintains the following basic records:

° The credit or loan file contains the loan application, financial statement, and general economic history of the subject.

° The liability ledger contains the customer liability to the bank at both the present time and at past times. These sheets also contain such information as the loan date, note number, amount of the loan, interest rate, due date, and payments.

° The collateral register usually contains a complete description of the items pledged as securities for loans. Records of such collateral can provide valuable information about a subject's assets.

CHECK CREDIT LOANS

Check credit is another loan service more and more banks are offering. Under a check credit plan the bank agrees to extend credit to a customer up to a maximum amount. The customer writes a check for any amount up to the maximum. If that amount is not in the checking account, the resulting overdraft is set up as a loan. The bank then bills the customer for the loan.

Another plan is a specialized checking account used only when checks are written up to a predetermined amount under a loan agreement; the outstanding balance is treated as an installment loan by the bank. Copies of loan agreements and statements for both plans can be obtained from the bank files.

CREDIT CARDS

Banks are doing an increasing business in credit cards. Under bank credit card plans, the cardholder can charge purchases at stores, restaurants, and other places that agree to accept the charges. In most plans the cardholder can elect to pay the entire balance in one payment or pay in installments under arrangements similar to an installment loan account. The charge plan records of importance to the economic crime investigator are the application for a card and the bank's copies of monthly statements sent to the cardholder. In some banks copies of the individual charges are also available. The monthly statements and/or individual charge documents listing the stores where the cardholder has made purchases can furnish valuable leads to the spending habits of the subject.

Most banks offering credit card plans are affiliated with a national credit card system.

SAFE-DEPOSIT BOXES

When banks rent safe-deposit boxes they are renting private vault space to customers. Since state laws differ, the nature of the relationship varies. Banks keep no record of the contents of safe-deposit boxes and generally do not know what the boxes contain.

The rental contract records identify the renters, the person or persons who have access to the boxes, their signatures, and the dates of the original agreements and later renewals and may contain other identifying information. Some contracts contain the name of the initiating bank officer. The officer's name could be significant if it is necessary to identify the subject (who may have used an alias in renting the box).

The records showing access to the boxes vary from bank to bank. They contain the signatures of the persons entering the boxes and usually the dates and times of entry. The entry records are filed in box number order.

The frequency of entry and the times and dates of entries may be significant and may correspond to the times and dates of deposits or withdrawals from other accounts or to the purchases and sales of securities, property, and so on.

OTHER SOURCES OF FINANCIAL INFORMATION: CREDIT AGENCIES

Local Credit-Reporting Associations

Most lines of business have local associations that may be contacted for information, such as jewelry retailers' association; jewelry manufacturers' association; building materials dealers' association; haberdashers' association; and grocers' association.

National Credit-Reporting Associations

These associations keep historical records of businesses including--

- ° Officers.

- ° Date of formation.

- ° Mergers or other changes in corporate structure.

- ° Data regarding sales, nature of business, to whom sales are made, that is, retailers, jobbers, wholesalers, and the like.

- ° Financial data including profit and loss statements and balance sheets where available.

- ° Published business ratio reports showing such key ratios in many industries and businesses by years as gross profit percentages earned, net profit to sales, and many others.

Retail Credit Associations (for individuals)

These associations keep the following information:

- ° Name, address, age, marital status, number of dependents.

- ° Occupation, employer, and salary.

- ° Firms who have made inquiry regarding credit status of individual (hence, firms with whom individual has done some business or has attempted to do business).

Telegraph Companies

Copies of telegrams and bank drafts are kept for 3 years. Transmittals of money exceeding $1000 are kept for 6 years.

Bonding Companies (financial statements)

Collateral as well as financial data to support the issuance of the bond should be on file.

INDIRECT METHODS OF TRACING FINANCIAL TRANSACTIONS

The income of a subject under investigation may be established by the direct or by the indirect approach. The direct approach, or specific-items method of proving income, relies upon specific transactions, such as sales or expenses, to determine income. The indirect approach relies upon circumstantial proof of income by the use of such methods as net worth, source and application of funds, and bank deposits.

Almost all individuals and business entities determine income by the specific items or specific transactions method. Most entities engaged in legitimate pursuits maintain books and records in which they record various transactions as they occur, and their computations of income are based upon the total of the transactions they engage in during the period. In economic crime investigations income usually can be established with less difficulty by the direct approach; for this reason, it should be used whenever possible.

In many investigations of economic crimes, however, a subject's books and records are not made available to the investigator. Therefore, an indirect approach must be taken using the net worth, source and application of funds, or bank deposit methods. Although these methods are considered circumstantial proof of income, the courts have approved their use in determining income for civil and criminal cases on the theory that proof of unexplained funds or property in the hands of a subject may establish a prima facie understatement of income.

NET WORTH METHOD

The net worth method is a frequently used indirect method of proving income from an unknown or illegal source. The method is presented in the familiar balance sheet format readily recognizable in the business world and presents a complete financial picture of a subject (see example, Net Worth Method of Computing Funds from Unknown or Illegal Sources). It is based on the theory that increases or decreases in a person's net worth during a period, adjusted for living expenses, result in a determination of income.

Net worth can be defined as the difference between a person's assets and liabilities at a particular point in time. By comparing the subject's net worth at the beginning and end of a period, usually a calendar year, the economic crime investigator can determine the subject's increase or decrease in net worth for the period. Adjustments are then made for living expenses to arrive at income. Income determined by this method includes receipts derived from all sources. Thus, by subtracting funds from known sources (salary, wages, interest, or dividends, for example), funds from unknown or illegal sources can be determined.

The courts have approved the use of the net worth method in numerous cases. Perhaps the leading Supreme Court case in this respect is Holland v. United States, 348 US 121 (1954), along with the three companion cases, Smith v. United States, 348 US 147 (1954); Friedberg v. United Statse, 348 142 (1954); and United States v. Calderon, 348 US 160 (1954). These cases outlined the broad principles governing the trial and review of cases based upon the net worth method of proving income.

	Net Worth 12/31/80 (base year)	12/31/81	12/31/82
ASSETS:			
Cash on hand	$ 100	$ —	$ —
Bank account balance	1,500	4,750	5,225
Jewelry	1,000	6,000	12,000
Boat	7,500	7,500	7,500
Automobile	—	—	13,250
Real estate	—	50,000	50,000
Total Assets	$10,100	$68,250	$87,975
LIABILITIES:			
Note payable—finance company	$ 275	$ 275	$ 275
Loan	—	2,400	1,200
Mortgage on real estate	—	36,400	32,800
Total Liabilities	$ 275	$39,075	$34,275
Net Worth	$ 9,825	$29,175	$53,700
Less: Prior year's net worth		9,825	29,175
Net worth increase (decrease)		$19,350	$24,525
Add: Personal living expenses			
Credit card payments		1,460	3,000
Other personal living expenses		11,000	10,000
Income		$31,810	$37,525
Less: Funds from known sources			
Interest on bank accounts		250	475
Wages		5,200	5,200
Total funds from known sources		5,450	5,675
Funds from unknown illegal sources		$26,360	$31,850

Net Worth Method of Computing Funds from Unknown or Illegal Sources

The formula for computing funds from unknown or illegal sources using the net worth method is as follows:

	Assets
Less:	Liablities
Equals:	Net worth
Less:	Prior years' net worth
Equals:	Net worth increase (decrease)
Less:	Living expenses
Equals:	Income (or expenditures)
Less:	Funds from known sources
Equals:	Funds from unknown/illegal sources

The net worth method is often used when several of the subject's assets and/or liabilities have changed during the period under investigation and one of the following conditions exists:

° The subject maintains no books and records.

° The subject's books and records are not available.

° The subject's books and records are inadequate.

° The subject withholds books and records.

An individual's assets, liabilities, and living expenses can be determined from a variety of sources, such as--

° The subject of the investigation.

° Informants' communications.

° Real estate records.

° Judgment and lien records.

° Bankruptcy records.

° State motor vehicle records.

° Loan applications.

° Financial statements.

° Accountant's workpapers.

° Surveillance.

° Credit card applications.

° Credit card statements.

° Tax returns.

° Insurance records.

° Child support and divorce records.

° Employment applications and salary checks.

° Companions of the subject.

° Canceled checks and deposited items.

In preparing a net worth statement, the question may arise of why items that do not change should be included in the net worth statement, particularly since these items have no bearing on the final result. It should be remembered that a net worth statement gives "a complete financial picture" of the subject.

Therefore, the statement should be as complete as possible so that the subject will not be able to contest its credibility on the ground that items were omitted. Additionally, the correct net worth statement may be the foundation for a future investigation of the subject, and a complete statement would prove extremely valuable at that time.

Cash on Hand

Cash on hand is coin and currency (bills, Federal Reserve notes, "greenbacks") in the subject's possession (on subject's person, in subject's residence or other place in nominee's hands, or in a safe deposit box). It does not include any money the subject has in any account with any type of financial institution.

When using the net worth method, the item most difficult to prove is cash on hand, which is usually claimed by defendants in sufficient amount to account for all or part of the unknown sources of income. To establish a firm starting net worth, it is necessary to show that the defendant had no large sum of cash for which he was not given credit. This is usually done by offering evidence that negates the existence of a cash hoard. Such evidence might be--

- Written or oral admissions of the subject to the investigating officers concerning net worth (for example, a signed net worth statement or an oral statement as to cash on hand).

- Low earnings in preprosecution years, as shown by records of former employers and/or tax returns filed by subject.

- Net worth, as established by books and records of the subject.

- Financial statement presented for credit or other purposes at a time before or during the period under investigation (banks, loan companies, and bonding companies are some of the better sources from which to obtain this type of document).

- Bankruptcy before prosecution periods.

- Prior indebtedness, compromise of overdue debts, and avoidance of bankruptcy.

- Installment buying.

- History of low earnings and expenditures, and checks returned for insufficient funds (a financial history covering members of the subject's family may also be helpful).

- Loss of furniture and business because of financial reasons.

- Receipt of some type of public assistance.

Living Expenses

Living expenses are expenditures made by a subject that technically are not classified as assets or liabilities. Living expenses include, but are not limited to, the following:

- Household expenses.
- Auto repairs.
- Insurance premiums.
- Contributions.
- Medical expenses.
- Taxes paid.
- Net gambling losses.
- Entertainment expenses.
- Gifts made to others.
- Losses on the sale of personal assets.

Funds from Known Sources

Funds from known sources include but are not limited to salaries, business profits, insurance proceeds, interest, dividends, inheritances, public assistance payments, tax refunds, and gifts received. Any loans that the subject received should not be included in this section if the loan was included in the computation as a liability (otherwise, the amount of the loan would be included twice).

The known sources of funds are subtracted from the determined income to arrive at funds from unknown or illegal sources.

SOURCES AND APPLICATION OF FUNDS METHOD

The source and application of funds method is an indirect method of determining unknown sources of funds and is often used by financial investigators because it is an easy method to understand and use.

The method is based on the theory that if expenditures for a given period exceed the subject's known sources of funds for that period, it may be inferred that the excess expenditures represent unknown or illegal income.

The source and application of funds method is a comparison of all known expenditures with all known receipts during a particular time period (see example below). When using this method, the economic crime investigator can determine where the subject's money came from (source) and what the subject did with the money (application). This method is known by various names, such as the expenditures method, flow of funds method, and statement of application of funds.

	Source and Application of Funds Statement	
	1981	1982
Application of Funds:		
Increase in bank balance	$ 3,250	$ 475
Purchase of jewelry	5,000	6,000
Down payment on residence	10,000	—
Purchase of automobile	—	13,250
Monthly mortgage payments	3,600	3,600
Credit card payments	1,460	3,000
Loan repayments	600	1,200
Other personal living expenses	11,000	10,000
Total application of funds	$34,910	$37,525
Less: Known sources of funds		
Cash on hand	100	—
Interest on bank account	250	475
Loan	3,000	—
Wages	5,200	5,200
Total known sources of funds	8,550	5,675
Funds from unknown or illegal sources	$26,360	$31,850

Source and Application of Funds Statement

The formula for computing funds from unknown or illegal sources using the source and application of funds method is as follows.

          Application of funds (expenditures)
Less: Known sources of funds
Equals: Funds from unknown or illegal sources

The statements made in discussing the net worth method with regard to when and how that method is used are also applicable to the source and application of funds method. In cases where the subject has several assets and liabilities whose cost basis remains the same throughout the period in which the economic crime investigator is interested, the expenditures method may be preferred over the net worth method because a briefer presentation can be made in the computation. Assets and liabilities that do not change during the period under investigation are omitted from the expenditures statement.

The source and application of funds method is used more often in cases where the subject's income is spent on lavish living and there is little, if any, net worth. Additionally, an expenditures statement can serve to verify the accuracy of another method of proving income and to test-check the accuracy of known or reported income. It can also be used to compute cash on hand for the base year of a net worth computation when a cash-on-hand starting point is found in a prior year.

In the source and application of funds method, the following items are considered in the computation:

° Application (expenditures).

- Increase in cash on hand or bank accounts.

- Increase in other assets (both personal and business).

- Decrease in liability balances.

- Personal living expenses.

° Known sources.

- Decreases in cash on hand or bank accounts.

- Sale or exchange of assets.

- Salaries or business profits.

- Tax refunds, interest, dividends, or insurance proceeds.

- Loans, gifts, or inheritances received.

- Unemployment or public assistance receipts.

- Other known sources.

Any excess of the application of funds over known sources of funds indicates funds from unknown or illegal sources.

It is imperative that the subject's cash on hand available at the beginning of the period is carefully tied down. Otherwise, the subject may contend that an accumulation of cash from previous periods was the source of funds expended during the period under investigation.

In many instances, however, the opening cash-on-hand figure cannot be readily determined. It may have to be computed from financial information obtained for years prior to the period under investigation. If information that dislosed the subject's cash on hand at some prior date is available, it may be possible to compute the subject's opening cash on hand by showing all sources of funds and their application during the interim period. The result of this computation would show the maximum amount of cash on hand that the subject could claim as a defense to either a net worth or expenditures computation.

BANK DEPOSITS METHOD

The bank deposits method is a means of proving unknown sources of funds by indirect or circumstantial evidence. Similar to the other indirect methods of proof, the bank deposits method computes income by showing what happened to a subject's funds.

The method is based on the theory that if a subject receives money, only two things can be done with the money--it can be deposited or it can be spent in the form of cash.

The bank deposits method is another means of proving unknown sources of funds by indirect or circumstantial evidence. By this method, income is proved through an analysis of bank deposits, canceled checks, and currency transactions of the subject (see chart on page 53). Adjustments for nonincome items are made to arrive at income.

A basic formula for the bank deposits method is as follows:

	Total deposits to all accounts
Less:	Transfer and redeposits
Equals:	Net deposits to all accounts
Plus:	Cash expenditures
Equals:	Total receipts from all sources
Less:	Funds from known sources
Equals:	Funds from unknown or illegal sources

The bank deposits method is recommended as a primary method of proof when most of the subject's income is deposited and the subject's books and records are--

° Unavailable.

° Withheld.

° Incomplete.

° Prepared with the bank deposits method.

	Bank Deposits		
		12/31/81	12/31/82
Total deposits		$22,160	$19,585
Less: Redeposits		660	100
Net deposits		$21,500	$19,485
Outlays:			
Purchase of jewelry	$ 5,000		$ 6,000
Down payment on residence	10,000		—
Purchase of automobile	—		13,250
Monthly mortgage payments	3,600		3,600
Credit card payment	1,460		3,000
Loan repayments	600		1,200
Other personal living expenses	11,000		10,000
Total outlays	$31,660		$37,050
Less: Net bank disbursements	18,250		19,010
Cash expenditures		13,410	18,040
Total receipts (income)		$34,910	$37,525
Less: Funds from known sources			
Cash on hand	$ 100		$ —
Interest on bank accounts	250		475
Loans	3,000		—
Wages	5,200		5,200
Total		8,550	5,675
Funds from unknown/illegal sources		$23,360	$31,850

Bank Deposits Computation of an Individual

The use of the bank deposits method is not limited to these circumstances. Even though the subject's books and records may appear complete and accurate, the method still can be used, and there is no requirement to disprove the accuracy of the books and records in order to do so.

The basic sources of information for the bank deposits computation are--

° Interview of subject.

° Analysis of the books and records.

° Analysis of the bank accounts.

A thorough interview is required to determine the subject's expenditures by cash and checks, to identify all of the subject's bank accounts, and to determine all loans and other receipts.

Total Deposits

Total deposits consist of not only amounts deposited to all bank accounts maintained or controlled by the subject but also deposits made to accounts in savings and loan companies, investment trusts, brokerage houses, and credit unions. Total deposits also include the accumulation (increase) of cash on hand. Since some subjects have bank accounts in fictitious names or under special titles, such as "Special Account No. 1," "Trustee Account," or "Trading Account," the investigator should inquire about this type of account during the investigation.

If a subject lists checks on a deposit ticket and deducts an amount paid to him in cash (split deposit), only the net amount of the deposit should be used in computing total deposits.

Additional items that must be included in deposits are property and notes that the subject received in payment for services rendered. Inasmuch as property and notes received in payment are income and must be accounted for in some manner, the accepted practice is to consider these items as forms of depositories into which funds have been placed for future use.

Net Deposits

All transfers or exchanges between bank accounts as well as funds that are redeposited are nonincome items and are subtracted from total deposits to arrive at net deposits. Failure to eliminate these items would result in an overstatement of income.

Cash Expenditures

Cash expenditures consist of the total outlay of funds less net bank disbursements, expressed as follows:

	Total outlay of funds
Less:	Net bank disbursements
Equals:	Cash bank disbursements

The total outlay of funds includes all payments made by cash or check. There is no need to determine which part was paid by cash and which part was paid by check. Total outlays include but are not limited to—

° Purchase of capital assets to investments (determined from settlement sheets, invoices, statements, and the like).

° Loan repayments (determined from loan ledgers of banks or other creditors).

° Living expenses (may be determined from the same sources presented in the net worth and expenditures sections).

  ° Purchases, business expenses (less non-flow-of-funds items, such as depreciation), rental expenses, and the like.

Net bank disbursements can be determined by the following formula:

	Net deposits to all accounts
Plus:	Beginning balances
Equals:	Net bank funds available
Less:	Ending balances
Equals:	Net banking disbursements

Funds from known sources include but are not limited to salaries, business profits, insurance proceeds, gifts received, loans received, and inheritances. Funds from known sources are subtracted from total receipts (or income) to arrive at funds from unknown or illegal sources.

STATISTICAL SAMPLING

Statistical sampling techniques can be used by a computer crime investigator for evaluating the record contents of large magnetic data case files. These techniques can be used to either prove guilty or exonerate a suspect.

Two basic methods of selecting samples are generally used by auditors and are in accordance with generally accepted auditing standards; judgment sampling and statistical sampling. Judgment sampling is any sample where the elements are selected subjectively rather than by random sampling.

Statistical sampling is a mathematical method of estimating value of population on the basis of samples from the population of interest.

Three types of sampling are defined below.

  ° Attributes Sampling (frequency estimation)

This method:

- is used to select records based on inconsistencies in characteristics within the record itself. It also can be used to test a population for the presence of particular characteristics.

- answers the question, "How many?"; does not measure dollars.

- is a useful tool for auditors to test compliance with pertinent accounting control procedures that leave an audit trail of evidence.

° Dollar Value Sampling (Variables Method)

This method:

- is used to estimate the total amount of a population or to decide whether the recorded amount may be materially misstated.

- answers the question, "How much?".

- is used for testing inventory amounts, testing the aging of accounts receivable balances, testing the adequacy of the allowance for bad debts, estimating the amout of a proposed accounting adjustment.

° Discovery Sampling (Exploratory)

This method:

- is intended to uncover the existence of errors.

- is sampling enough to conclude either that a stipulated condition does not exist or to find an example.

- answers the question, "How many items must be examined so that if the occurrence rate exceeds a critical value there is a stipulated probability of observing an occurrence in the sample?".

- is often a useful technique to use in conjunction with populations that ordinarily have low occurrence rates such as bank demand deposits.

MAIN ADVANTAGES OF STATISTICAL SAMPLING

A more objective method is provided in the determination of sampling risks, the sample size, and the evaluation of the sample.

When judgment sampling is used by the auditor, acceptable error limits and reliability levels are kept in mind, but no specific values are assigned to them. If a higher degree of reliability is desired or fewer errors are responsible, the number of items tested must be increased. However, the auditor cannot determine, through judgment sampling, how many items to sample in order to attain a specific degree of reliability, and degree of reliability cannot be determined after selecting and examining the sample. Furthermore, the auditor cannot measure the accuracy of the sample estimate.

With statistical sampling, the auditor is able to determine objectively how many items must be sampled to attain a certain confidence level and a desired degree of precision. This advance sample-size determination is an approximation based on mathematical formulas which take into consideration factors of internal control, materiality of errors, and the nature of sample items. Statistical sampling, therefore, enables the auditor to state quantitatively the risk he is assuming.

Typically, the auditor is required to plan his approach in a more orderly manner than is common when judgment sampling is employed.

When the population is relatively large, a statistical sample might be smaller than a judgment sample, thereby saving time and reducing cost.

As the population increases in size, the sample size required for the same confidence level and degree of precision will increase somewhat, but not proportionately to the increase in population. This is a major efficiency of statistical sampling.

Statistical samples may be combined and evaluated, even though selected and examined by different auditors. For example, in an audit covering a number of locations, the audit can be performed independently and separately at the different locations and the results combined for an overall evaluation of all locations if statistical techniques have been applied.